This book belongs to

Stephanie

MY VERY FIRST
BOOK OF

BIBLE
WORDS

Copyright © 1993 by Educational Publishing Concepts, Inc., Wheaton, Illinois

Published in Nashville, Tennessee, by Oliver-Nelson Books, a division of Thomas Nelson, Inc., Publishers and distributed in Canada by Word Communications, Ltd., Richmond, British Columbia.

The Bible version used in this publication is THE NEW KING JAMES VERSION. Copyright © 1979, 1980, 1982, Thomas Nelson, Inc., Publishers.

Printed in the United States of America.

Library of Congress Cataloging-in-Publication Data

Hollingsworth, Mary, 1947—
      My very first book of Bible words / Mary Hollingsworth.
            p.   cm.
      Summary: Includes illustrations, brief definitions, quotes from the Bible, and activities to demonstrate the meaning of such words as "family," "prayer," "obey," "worship," "church," and "love."
      ISBN 0-8407-9226-3 (hardcover)
      1. Children—Religious life. 2. Bible—Juvenile literature.
   3. Activity programs in Christian education. [1. Christian life.
   2. Vocabulary.] I. Title
BV4571.2.H67   1993
242'.62—dc20   9321843
                                                                CIP
                                                                 AC

1 2 3 4 5 6 — 98 97 96 95 94 93

MY VERY FIRST BOOK OF

BIBLE WORDS

Mary Hollingsworth

Illustrated by
Rick Incrocci

THOMAS NELSON PUBLISHERS
Nashville

Dear Parents,

Words, words, words! This book is all about words. But not just any old words. No, indeed! These are words from the Bible, so they are the most important words in the world for your child to learn.

One of the best things about this book is how easy it is to understand. All your child has to do is learn one word each time you turn the page. And there are pictures and things to do to make the learning even easier.

If your child can read, she can learn these wonderful words all by herself. That's great! If your child can't read yet, you can help him learn the words. The questions and things to do will let you interact with your child to implant these important words in your child's heart for life.

Just turn the page to learn the first great word from God. And have fun!

Mary Hollingsworth

Turn to the LORD your God and
obey His voice.

Deuteronomy 4:30

Obey

To Learn:

To *obey* means to do what someone
asks you to do. Whom should you
obey? (God, parents, teachers.)

To Do:

Draw a picture of yourself doing
something your mom or dad asked you
to do.

OBEY

O LORD my God, in You I
put my trust.

Psalm 7:1

Trust

To Learn:

To *trust* means to depend on someone
or something. Whom can you trust?
(God, parents, relatives, teachers,
caregivers.)Whom does the boy in the
picture trust? (God.)

To Do:

Hug someone you love and trust right
now.

TRUST

The word of the LORD is right.

Psalm 33:4

Bible

To Learn:

The *Bible* is the Word of the Lord.
It tells us how to live and be happy.
Do you have a Bible of your very own?

To Do:

Sing "The B-I-B-L-E" with someone.

BIBLE

In You, O LORD, I hope.
Psalm 38:15

Hope

To Learn:

Hope means you want and expect
something to happen. You hope your
birthday will come really soon. You
hope you will get lots of presents.

To Do:

Point to the lost boy in the picture.
What does he hope will happen? (He
will find his way home.)

HOPE

Sing praises to God, sing praises!

Psalm 47:6

Sing

To Learn:

When you *sing*, you make music with your voice. God says singing will make us happy. The children in the picture look happy to be singing. What is your favorite song about God?

To Do:

Sing "Jesus Loves Me" right now.

SING

Make His praise glorious!

Psalm 66:2

Praise

To Learn:

Praise is telling God how much we love and worship Him. The girl in the picture is praising God by painting a picture.

To Do:

Praise God in a way you enjoy; sing a song, say verse, paint a picture.

PRAISE

God sets the solitary in families.

Psalm 68:6

Family

To Learn:

A *family* is a group of people who love and care for one another. God made families so we would not have to be alone. Who are the people in your family? (Mom, dad, brother, sister, grandparents, others.)

To Do:

Draw a picture of your family. Ask your mom or dad to hang it in your room.

FAMILY

He shall give His angels
charge over you.

Psalm 91:11

Angel

To Learn:

An *angel* is a helper from God. Angels take care of us. How is the angel in this picture taking care of the boy? (By holding him and reading to him.)

To Do:

If you were an angel, what would you do for your mom and dad?

ANGEL

My help comes from the LORD.
Psalm 121:2

Help

To Learn:

When you do something for others,
you *help* them. Friends and family
always help each other. How is the
angel helping the girl? (By pushing the
stone up the hill.)

To Do:

Make a list of three things you can do
to help your family.

HELP

Happy are the people whose
God is the LORD!

Psalm 144:15

Happy

To Learn:

People who are *happy* are glad or pleasec
God says you will be happy when you dc
good things for other people. Why are
the two girls in this picture happy?
(They are doing something good.)

To Do:

Ask your mom or dad to help you make
a nice card. Mail it to someone who
needs to be cheered up.

HAPPY

The LORD . . . hears the prayer
of the righteous.

Proverbs 15:29

Prayer

To Learn:

Prayer is talking to God. The Bible says
God listens to our prayers. Do you
think God heard the prayer of the boy?
(Yes.) Why? (It is raining.)

To Do:

Talk to God right now. Thank Him for
His Son Jesus who came to save you.

PRAYER

[There is] a time to laugh.

Ecclesiastes 3:4

Laugh

To Learn:

Your *laugh* is a sound that shows how happy you are. God loves to hear you laugh. That is how He knows you are happy to be His child. What funny things make you laugh? Why do you think the children in this picture are laughing?

To Do:

Pretend someone is tickling you right now. Laugh as hard as you can.

LAUGH

[There is] a time to dance.

Ecclesiastes 3:4

Dance

To Learn:

To *dance* means to move your body to music or in rhythm. Dancing for God is another way we show Him how happy we are to be like Him. Why do you think the girl in this picture is dancing?

To Do:

While God watches from heaven, dance for Him by yourself. Show Him how much you love Him.

DANCE

Learn to do good.

Isaiah 1:17

Learn

To Learn:

When we get to know or understand
something, we *learn* it. God wants us to
know more and more about how to do
good things as we grow up. What good
thing is the boy in the picture learning?
(To take care of his grandmother.)

To Do:

Draw a picture of yourself doing
something you want to learn to do.

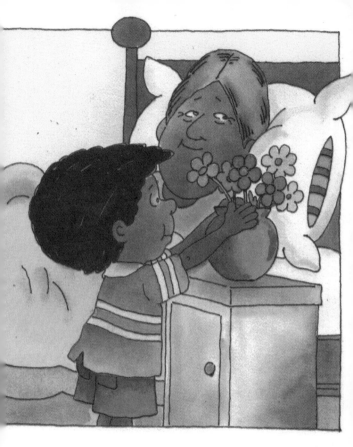

LEARN

You shall worship the LORD your God.
Matthew 4:10

Worship

To Learn:

Worship is what we say or do to honor and praise God. We worship God when we tell Him how much we love Him. We worship when we thank Him for all He gives us.

To Do:

Worship God right now by singing "Oh How I Love Jesus."

WORSHIP

Blessed are the peacemakers.

Matthew 5:9

Peace

To Learn:

Peace is when people are happy to be together. How can you tell when two people do not have peace? (They fight.)

To Do:

Tear a sheet of paper into pieces. Put it back together. That is like making peace between friends who are fighting.

PEACE

Rejoice and be . . . glad, for great is your reward in heaven.

Heaven

To Learn:

Heaven is a wonderful place where God's children live forever with Him. Jesus said we will all live in mansions in heaven. Would you like to live in a mansion in heaven?

To Do:

Draw a picture of the beautiful mansion in heaven where you would like to live.

HEAVEN

His [Jesus'] disciples followed Him.

Matthew 8:23

Disciple

To Learn:

A *disciple* follows or learns to be like a teacher. The Bible says we should all learn to be like Jesus, the master teache

To Do:

Play Follow the Leader with your dad o mom. You be the disciple.

DISCIPLE

Jesus said, "Let the little children
come to Me."

Matthew 19:14

Children

To Learn:

Children are young people like yourself.
Jesus loves children very much. He loves
all children. He loves your laughter and
happy smile. He loves your prayers and
songs. He loves for you to do good
things. Jesus loves you!

To Do:

Sing "Jesus Loves the Little Children of
the World."

CHILDREN

Go . . . and make disciples
of all the nations.

Matthew 28:19

Go

To Learn:

We *go* when we move to another place.
God loves for us to go new places. And
He wants us to tell other people about
Him. What are the children in this
picture doing? (Going on a mission
trip.)

To Do:

Name a place you sometimes go. What
can you do to tell people about God
when you go there next time?

GO

Repent, and believe in the gospel.
Mark 1:15

Gospel

To Learn:

The *gospel* is the good news about Jesus' coming to save us. The good news is in the Bible. How are these children sharing the gospel? (By sending Bibles to others.)

To Do:

Point to the Bibles in the picture. Whom would you like to send a Bible to?

GOSPEL

Go into all the world and preach the
gospel to every creature.

Mark 16:15

Preach

To Learn:

To *preach* means to tell other people
the good news about Jesus. Which
person in this picture is the preacher?
(The woman with the Bible.) Which
person is the learner? (The gang
member.)

To Do:

Pretend you are a preacher. Tell the
good news of Jesus to your mom and
dad.

PREACH

Love one another.

John 13:34

Love

To Learn:

To *love* others is to like them and respect them. We love God. We love our families. And we love our friends. Love is the best feeling in the world.

To Do:

Love is also something we do. Make a present for someone you love. Give it to the person.

LOVE

Many wonders and signs were done through the apostles.

Acts 2:43

Apostle

To Learn:

An *apostle* was a special follower of Jesus. Jesus chose twelve men to be His apostles. They preached the good news about Jesus to the whole world. Can you name one of the apostles?

To Do:

Point to the apostle in this picture. Why is the boy dancing? (He has been healed.)

APOSTLE

I believe that Jesus Christ is the
Son of God.

Acts 8:37

Believe

To Learn:

To *believe* something means that you
trust it is true. The Bible says Jesus is
the Son of God. Do you believe that is
true? (Yes.) Why? (The Bible says it is
true.)

To Do:

Draw a picture of Jesus and God, His
Father.

BELIEVE

The disciples were first called Christians in Antioch.

Acts 11:26

Christian

To Learn:

The word *Christian* means someone who believes and follows Jesus Christ. It lets others know what we believe. Do you think the people in this picture are Christians? (Yes.) Why? (They are praying.)

To Do:

Ask your mom or dad to help you print the word *Christian* on a shirt.

CHRISTIAN

The disciples were filled with joy and
with the Holy Spirit.

Acts 13:52

Holy Spirit

To Learn:

The *Holy Spirit* is God living in us. Jesus
said the Holy Spirit comforts us when
we are hurt. He is our friend and teache
He makes us happy. Do you think these
children know the Holy Spirit? (Yes.)
Why? (They are happy.)

To Do:

Make up a song to sing about your
friend, the Holy Spirit.

HOLY SPIRIT

God worked unusual miracles.

Acts 19:11

Miracle

To Learn:

A *miracle* is something wonderful that God does. The girl in the picture can not see. What is Jesus doing for her? (Helping her see.) That is a miracle!

To Do:

Pretend you can do miracles. What miracle will you do?

MIRACLE

It is more blessed to give than
to receive.

Acts 20:35

Give

To Learn:

To *give* is to let someone have what is yours. The Bible says you will be happier when you give gifts than when you get gifts. It is fun to see people smile when you give them gifts. Have you given someone a gift? Tell about it.

To Do:

Make a gift for someone you love. Give it to the person with a hug.

GIVE

And the God of peace will
crush Satan.

Romans 16:20

Satan

To Learn:

Satan is God's enemy. He is evil and
mean. Satan wants to steal you from
Jesus. He wants you to be bad, just like
him.

To Do:

Ask God to help you act like Jesus.
Ask Him to help you fight Satan.

SATAN

For the message of the cross . . . is
the power of God.

1 Corinthians 1:18

Cross

To Learn:

A *cross* is two pieces of wood that form
a *t*. God loves you so much that He let
Jesus die on a cross for you. That is the
saddest thing that ever happened. But
it is also the happiest thing that ever
happened because now you can be
saved!

To Do:

Bow your head and sing the song
"Thank You, Lord."

CROSS

Care for one another.

1 Corinthians 12:25

Care

To Learn:

When we *care* for people, we want them to be well and happy. What is wrong with the boy in the picture? (He is sick. How is the young doctor taking care of him? (By seeing if he has a fever.)

To Do:

Write a letter to someone you know who is unhappy or sick. Tell the person you care and hope he or she gets better soon.

CARE

Through love serve one another.

Galatians 5:13

Serve

To Learn:

To *serve* others means you help them. How is the waiter in this picture serving his friends? (By serving dinner.)

To Do:

Ask your mom or dad to let you help serve dinner for your family.

SERVE

For by grace you have been saved
through faith.

Ephesians 2:8

Grace

To Learn:

Grace is God's kindness to us. God's
grace lets us be saved and live with Him
in heaven. God's grace protects us from
harm. Are these children enjoying God'
grace? (Yes.) Does God's grace protect
you when you sleep, too? (Yes.)

To Do:

Talk to God right now. Thank Him for
His wonderful grace.

GRACE

At the name of Jesus every knee
should bow.

Philippians 2:10

Jesus

To Learn:

Jesus is the Son of God. He is the Lord
of heaven and earth. He is our Savior
and friend. We should always worship
Jesus. Are these children worshiping
Him? (Yes.)

To Do:

Get down on your knees. Tell Jesus
how much you love Him.

JESUS

Work with your own hands.
1 Thessalonians 4:11

Work

To Learn:

To *work* is to use your energy to do a task. God gave us work to do on the earth. Work keeps us busy and happy as God's children. How are the children in this picture working? (By planting flowers.)

To Do:

Ask your mom or dad to help you work in your yard.

WORK

Take care of the church of God.

1 Timothy 3:5

Church

To Learn:

The *church* is God's family. We are all
brothers and sisters in God's family.
God loves and protects the people in
His church. Do you like to go to
church?

To Do:

Draw a picture of two people who are
in the church where you go.

CHURCH

Let them do good, that they be . . .
willing to share.

1 Timothy 6:18

Share

To Learn:

When you *share*, you give another
person part of what you have. You can
share your toys, your food, and your
time. Are the children in this picture
sharing? (Yes.)

To Do:

Ask your mom or dad to give you two
cookies. Share one of the cookies with
someone else.

SHARE

You should follow His steps.

1 Peter 2:21

Follow

To Learn:

The word *follow* means to try to be like another person. We should always follow Jesus or try to be like Him. What is the girl in the picture doing? (Following the steps.)

To Do:

Jesus helped people. Follow Jesus by helping your mom or dad clean the house today.

FOLLOW

God is love.

1 John 4:8

God

To Learn:

God is the Creator and Ruler of everything. God gave us life and love. He gave us Jesus to save us from our sins. The Bible says God is love. We should show love to people as God does.

To Do:

Cut a heart out of a piece of paper. Write "God loves you" on the heart. Give the heart to someone you love.

GOD

Other books in this series

My Very First Book of Bible Lessons

My Very First Book of Prayers

My Very First Book of Bible Heroes